HONEST, HEALED, & HAPPY

LESLIE BOLES-MUHAMMAD

DEDICATION

To my son, Tristan Barker, whose light inspires me to shine brighter every day—may this work remind you that authentic joy comes from embracing your true self.

And to my husband, Antar Muhammad, whose unwavering support and love create the space where I can be honest, healed, and truly happy—thank you for walking this path with me.

Your presence in my life is the greatest testament to God's faithfulness and grace.

CONTENTS

DEVOTION DAY 1:
THE PROCESS OF GREATNESS

The biggest tree in any yard or park started as a seed. The adult "you" is proof of that. Each of us began as an embryo in our mother's womb and has grown into the body we have today. We live in a society where we believe that greatness happens instantly because of viral videos and microwave ovens when, in reality, that is typically not how success works.

I once heard Daymond John say, "Every overnight success takes a minimum of fifteen years." I don't know about you, but Daymond John's words were liberating for me. I began to change my philosophy, and hopefully, my newfound freedom will deliver you, too! Starting today, for twenty-one days in total, we will do the work to help you construct the best version of yourself. You do not have to wait until next month or next year. You can start today.

We are taking all the limits and time frames off! No more putting age limits on our goals, dreams, and destiny. Now, I believe that we should set targeted deadlines. However, if you get off track, all will not be lost. You will reset and get back on track. Very few people had successfully achieved all their goals by the time they believed they would be achieved. Yet, unless a goal is completely abandoned, it can and will still be reached because greatness takes time! And I know, without a shadow of a doubt, you and I were destined to be great.

As we take this journey together, I want you to guard your gates. Please be mindful of negative self-talk and dysfunctional or toxic environments. I would love for you to be intentional about taking this journey. Today, I am going to share a short story about someone whose journey to greatness had a lot of twists and turns.

Devotional Scripture Day 1
1 Samuel 16:1-3, NIV

"1 The Lord said to Samuel, "How long will you mourn for Saul since I have rejected him as king over Israel? Fill your horn with oil and be on your way; I am sending you to Jesse of Bethlehem. I have chosen one of his sons to be king." 2 But Samuel said, "How can I go? If Saul hears about it, he will kill me." The Lord said, "Take a heifer with you and say, 'I have come to sacrifice to the Lord.'
3 Invite Jesse to the sacrifice, and I will show you what to do. You are to anoint for me the one I indicate."

According to Biblestudy.org, "the historian Josephus says that David was ten years old when anointed; modern commentaries place the age at around fifteen. David began to rule when the tribe of Judah asked him to reign over them when he was about thirty years old. After about seven and one-half years, the remaining tribes of Israel acknowledge him as the sole ruler. Conservatively, the period between when he was anointed and officially began to rule was fifteen years." There is Daymond John's "fifteen-year" reference number again. Yet, David's story of greatness is significant for more reasons than just how long it took him to take his rightful place on the throne.

First, David was **overlooked**. David's own father did not consider that he could be the next king of Israel. He was the youngest of eight children, and he had to be "fetched" even to get an opportunity to be seen by the prophet. However, we can learn a lot through David's story, including that God's vision for your life supersedes what others around you (even family) can see.

Next, David was **underestimated**. When Goliath was shouting his obscenities against the soldiers of Israel, David stood up and challenged Goliath. David's brothers thought he was trying to be funny, and Saul dismissed him at first, too. When Saul realized he was serious, he tried to give David his armor. David declined. He had his own weapons: a slingshot, and five smooth stones.

In the end, David was **undefeated** and eventually was anointed king. He did not get there by accident. There was a process that led to his greatness.

The elimination of the process, stress, and struggle frustrates me about some memoirs that only string together the highlight reel of the best events of the author's life. We need more transparent, authentic stories that start at the beginning. We need people to tell the whole truth and nothing but the truth about the infancy stage and the development that followed that led to the peaks and valleys of greatness.

I encourage you to do what I am going to do when I get there. I will talk about my complete journey, and I assure you I will not just tell stories about specific moments. I want to encourage you as I encourage myself; you are on your way to greatness. Your process is unique. It is unlike your mother's, sister's, best friend's, or mine. God has a pre-destined path marked just for you. I am cheering you on as you go!

Devotional Downloads

You will need four mindsets to assist you on the path to greatness:

1. **Growth mindset:** embrace challenges and view failures as opportunities to learn and improve.
2. **Resilience mindset:** persevere through setbacks and obstacles and maintain a positive attitude.
3. **Innovative mindset:** think outside the box and approach problems with an open mind.
4. **Transformation mindset:** focus on positively impacting others and the world around you.

Which of these mindsets would be most helpful for you to adopt during this phase of your life?

_____

_____

_____

_____

_____

_____

How can you implement it today in your daily life?

_____

_____

_____

_____

_____

_____

Who can you tag to hold you accountable for aggressively pursuing this necessary mindset shift in your life?

_____

_____

_____

_____

_____

_____

Honest, Healed, & Happy

DEVOTION DAY 2:
SMALL BEGINNINGS

It is easy to get discouraged when we are faced with small beginnings. We may feel like our efforts are not making a significant impact or that we are not making progress as quickly as we would like. However, the Bible reminds us that God always watches over us, even in the small things. He is present in every step we take toward our goals, and He is using those moments to teach us and mold us into the person He wants us to be.

In the book of Zechariah, we see the prophet Zerubbabel tasked with rebuilding the temple in Jerusalem. It was a massive undertaking, and the progress was slow at first. But God encouraged Zerubbabel, saying, "Do not despise these small beginnings, for the Lord rejoices to see the work begin" (Zechariah 4:10, NLT). God knew that each step was necessary to achieve the end goal, and He was pleased to see the work begin.

We can apply this lesson to our own lives. We should not be discouraged by small beginnings or feel like our efforts are insignificant. Every step we take toward our goals is important, no matter how small it may seem. It is essential to trust in God's plan for our lives and to know that He is using every moment to teach us and prepare us for what is to come.

Then, sometimes, our small beginnings take us on a path that resembles a pit and/or a prison before reaching our palace or Promised Land. That is what happened to Joseph. Let's dive into today's Scripture lesson.

Devotional Scripture Day 2
Genesis 45:4-8, NLT

"4 Please, come closer," he said to them. So they came closer.
And he said again, "I am Joseph, your brother, whom you sold
into slavery in Egypt. 5 But don't be upset and don't be angry
with yourselves for selling me to this place. It was God who sent
me here ahead of you to preserve your lives.
6 This famine that has ravaged the land for two years will last
five more years, and there will be neither plowing nor
harvesting. 7 God has sent me ahead of you to keep you and your
families alive and to preserve many survivors.
8 So it was God who sent me here, not you! And he is the one who
made me an adviser to Pharaoh—the manager of his entire
palace and the governor of all of Egypt."

If you grew up in church or went to Sunday School, you are all too familiar with the story of Joseph. If you didn't but had small kids in early 2000, you may have seen Dreamwork's animated feature film, *Joseph: King of Dreams*. Either way, Joseph's account is a popular one. As his father's favorite son, Joseph is so adored by his dad that he gives him a "coat of many colors." Joseph's inability to "read the room," as we would say today, created a devastating chain of events for the young man.

First, he shared a dream with his family that had all of them bowing down to him. He gave too much information to the wrong people. His brothers were so angry with him that they plotted to kill him. But, at the last minute, his brother Judah saved his life by suggesting they sell him into slavery instead.

Next, while serving as a slave, he prospered in his master's house. He learned Egyptian customs and language and excelled in every way. He was such a standout that he ended up on the radar of his master's wife, and when he refused her advances, she accused him of assault. His integrity and character resulted in his being thrown into prison.

In prison, he excelled again. Everywhere Joseph went, no matter how small his station or position, he made it better. While imprisoned, he ended up interpreting dreams for two prisoners. Later, when the Pharaoh had a dream that no one in the land could decipher, the former prisoner remembered Joseph. Joseph was able to interpret the dream and was promoted to second in command.

One of Joseph's main jobs was to plan for a famine that he foresaw in his dream. Sure enough, when the famine came to pass, Joseph's brothers ended up in Egypt to secure food for themselves and their elderly parents. After a series of encounters, Joseph reveals himself to them in our devotional Scripture lesson.

Joseph's revelation is not one of bitter ranting and raving. It is a testimony of the goodness of God's vision.

1. He told them not to be angry with themselves.
2. He let them know that God sent him ahead of them to preserve all their lives.

3. His small beginning led him to a big position as the governor over all of Egypt.

Similarly, many African Americans are descendants of slavery. That is often the simplest and smallest, lowest beginning imaginable. Yet, today, we as a people have achieved success that our ancestors couldn't even have imagined for us. Today, let us learn to embrace small beginnings and trust in God's plan for our lives. Let us be patient and persistent, knowing that every step counts towards our success. As we focus on the journey, we can learn valuable lessons that will help us grow and achieve our goals. Let us remember that God is always with us and rejoices in every step we take toward fulfilling His purpose for our lives.

Devotional Downloads

Starting small and celebrating early wins is much easier said than done. It can be challenging when you are at the beginning of anything new. There are four keys I want to share with you to do in the "Small Beginnings" season:

1. **Identify your support system**: reach out to friends, family, or a therapist to talk about what you're going through.

2. **Stay positive**: focus on the good things in your life and work to maintain a positive outlook.

3. **Select or resume a hobby or recreational activity**: give yourself permission to take breaks and do things you enjoy to help reduce stress and improve your mood.

4. **Seek help if needed**: if you're struggling to cope, don't hesitate to seek professional help from a pastor, therapist, or counselor.

List your support system here:

_____

_____

_____

_____

_____

What brings you joy and helps you remain positive? Make a note of it here.

_____

_____

_____

_____

_____

Jot down a current list of hobbies and recreational activities; if you don't have any, make a list of things you will start this weekend!

_____

_____

_____

_____

Mental health is critical. If you are struggling with feelings of anxiety, stress, depression, or overwhelm, please seek help from a trained and trusted professional or check out this list of resources from the National Council for Mental Wellbeing: https://www. mentalhealthfirstaid.org/mental-health-resources/

DEVOTION DAY 3:
FOLLOW YOUR INSTINCTS

One of the greatest lessons we can learn in life is the importance of following our instincts, especially when we face failures. It's easy to become overwhelmed by our emotions when we fail; sometimes, it feels like giving up is the only way to escape the pain. But successful people know that true success is achieved by persevering through the failures, and that requires following our instincts even when our emotions are telling us to quit.

When we follow our instincts, we tap into a deeper wisdom that comes from our inner selves. It's the knowledge that can't be taught but is learned through experience, trial, and error. When we trust our instincts, we permit ourselves to take risks, try new things, and learn from our mistakes. We may not always get it right, but we can always learn from and grow from our failures.

The Bible tells us that faith is the substance of things hoped for, the evidence of things not seen (Hebrews 11:1). We may not always know the way forward, but if we follow our instincts and have faith that we will succeed, then we will overcome our failures and achieve our goals. One way we can tap into our instincts is by listening to the prompting of God. Today, we rely on the Spirit of God to lead and guide us the same way people did during the Biblical era.

Devotional Scripture Day 3
2 Kings 4:18-25, ESV

*"18 When the child had grown, he went out one day to
his father among the reapers. 19 And he said to his father,
"Oh, my head, my head!" The father said to his servant, "Carry
him to his mother." 20 And when he had lifted him and
brought him to his mother, the child sat on her lap till noon, and
then he died. 21 And she went up and laid him on the bed of the
man of God and shut the door behind him and went out.
22 Then she called to her husband and said, "Send me one of the
servants and one of the donkeys, that I may quickly go to the
man of God and come back again." 23 And he said, "Why will
you go to him today? It is neither new moon nor Sabbath." She
said, "All is well." 24 Then she saddled the donkey, and she said
to her servant, "Urge the animal on; do not slacken the pace for
me unless I tell you." 25 So she set out and came to the man of
God at Mount Carmel. When the man of God saw her coming,
he said to Gehazi, his servant, "Look, there is the Shunammite."*

Today's Scripture lesson is an incredible example of a woman
who knew how to follow her instincts. The Shunammite woman
was a previously barren woman who was a gracious host to the
prophet Elisha and his servant. She built a guest room for them in
her house with her husband's permission. Elisha was so taken
with her hospitality that he had his servant investigate a way to
repay her kindness. Gehazi (his servant) let him know that she was
childless. Elisha prayed and prophesied to her, saying, "About this
time next season, you will hold a son."

The prophet's words came to pass, and against all odds, the Shunammite woman became a mother to a little boy.

Our Scripture lesson picks up here. The little boy is outside in the field with his father, grows ill, and faints. His father instinctively sends him to his mother. His mother immediately seeks out the prophet. Everyone is following their instincts in the story. The mother's ability to fight off her emotions, stay calm, and get to the man of God who facilitated her blessing in the first place—saved her son's life. I encourage you to read the rest of the story at your leisure.

The Shunammite gives a masterclass in following instincts in the midst of turbulent, unthinkable situations. The beauty of the modern-day believer is that we no longer have to seek a priest or prophet to pray to God on our behalf as she did. We can humbly go before the throne of grace for ourselves. The key is knowing when to apply faith, when to activate works, and when to combine the two.

So today, let us commit to following our instincts, even when we face failure. Let us have faith that our instincts will guide us on the right path and that success is just around the corner. Let us not be discouraged by our failures but use them as opportunities to learn and grow. And above all, let us trust in God's plan for our lives, knowing that He will guide us through every success and every failure. Amen.

Devotional Downloads

I have found a few ways to help you follow your instincts.

1. **Listen to your body**: your body is constantly sending you signals and messages about what it needs. Learn to pay attention to these signals and listen to your body's needs.

2. **Trust your gut**: your gut instinct is often more accurate than you think. If something doesn't feel right, trust that feeling and take action accordingly.

3. **Practice mindfulness**: mindfulness can help you tune into your instincts and become more aware of your thoughts and feelings. Take time daily to practice mindfulness and become more in tune with yourself.

Out of three ways to help you follow your instincts more freely, which ones will be the most helpful for you?

_____

_____

_____

_____

_____

_____

How can you implement this practice in your day-to-day life?

_____

_____

_____

_____

_____

_____

Record a situation where you wish you had followed your instincts but did not. What lesson did you learn?

_____

_____

_____

_____

_____

Honest, Healed, & Happy

DEVOTION DAY 4:
MENTAL ACROBATICS - ELIMINATING FALSE FACTS

"Our deepest fear is not that we are inadequate. Our deepest fear is that we are powerful beyond measure. It is our light, not our darkness, that most frightens us. We ask ourselves, 'Who am I to be brilliant, gorgeous, talented, fabulous?' Actually, who are you not to be? You are a child of God. Your playing small does not serve the world. There is nothing enlightened about shrinking so that other people won't feel insecure around you. We are all meant to shine, as children do. We were born to manifest the glory of God that is within us. It's not just in some of us; it's in everyone. And as we let our own light shine, we unconsciously give other people permission to do the same. As we are liberated from our own fear, our presence automatically liberates others."
**—Marianne Williamson, A Return to Love:
Reflections on the Principles of A Course in Miracles**

This quote has become one of my favorites; it is from a 1992 self-help book by Marianne Williamson. Let's take time to break it down. We see an excellent manifesto for children of God, and specifically daughters of the King.

When she addresses "deepest fears," I can relate. Often, when I assumed I was afraid of failing, in all actuality, I was terrified of success. After all, achieving success is not a one-in-done deal. Think about some of your favorite artists who have been reduced to being described as a "one-hit-wonder!" Success requires work to get there and even more to remain.

I want to encourage you to refrain from letting the work required to succeed scare you out of shining. Equally important, you must shine regardless of who it bothers or offends. After all, God cannot get the glory out of your life if you are constantly hiding and running from the power you possess from within. It is time for God to get the glory out of your life because your light invites others to release theirs. Your decision to unshackle yourself from the chains of fear, low self-esteem, and self-doubt can simultaneously be the key to unlocking someone else's shackles.

Now, if you are wondering, "Leslie, will I just wake up one day and have confidence?" I can tell you honestly, "No. Often, the first step you take is 'doing it afraid." Some of the most outstanding leaders of all time begin their journeys doubting their abilities, even those called by God directly. I can give you an example: Moses.

In your leisure, I encourage you to read about Moses's entire life, specifically Exodus 3 and 4. I highlight these chapters because they are in the middle of Moses's life. Moses' early life is referenced a great deal. His mom had to put him in a basket on the Nile River to save his life from the very Pharaoh's house he ended up living with (being raised by the ruler's daughter). He lived among the Egyptians until he discovered the truth about his heritage. Soon after that, Moses saw an Egyptian mistreating a fellow Hebrew. Moses killed him and fled Egypt.

The next thing we hear about is the plagues, Moses' famous line: "Let my people go," and his parting of the Red Sea during the enslaved Hebrew people's escape. Yet, in between Moses going into hiding and becoming one of the most famous leaders of the Old Testament, he felt inadequate and basically told God the equivalent of the social media meme that is being popularly quoted at the time of this writing, "Get somebody else to do it."

As humorous as that may be to us in the modern world, let's break down Moses' life up to this point. First, he should have been dead. Pharaoh had decreed that all Hebrew male babies be put to death. Yet, the midwives feared God and devised a cover story. We see the story unfold before Moses' birth in Exodus 1.

Devotional Scripture Day 4
Exodus 1:15-22, NIV

"15 The King of Egypt said to the Hebrew midwives, whose names were Shiphrah and Puah, 16 "When you are helping the Hebrew women during childbirth on the delivery stool, if you see that the baby is a boy, kill him; but if it is a girl, let her live."
17 The midwives, however, feared God and did not do what the King of Egypt had told them to do; they let the boys live.
18 Then the King of Egypt summoned the midwives and asked them, "Why have you done this? Why have you let the boys live?" 19 The midwives answered Pharaoh, "Hebrew women are not like Egyptian women; they are vigorous and give birth before the midwives arrive." 20 So God was kind to the midwives, and the people increased and became even more numerous.
21 And because the midwives feared God, he gave them families of their own. 22 Then Pharaoh gave this order to all his people: "Every Hebrew boy that is born you must throw into the Nile, but let every girl live."

Devotional Downloads

Let this be a lesson to all of us that:

1. **God has a plan for each of us before we are even conceived.**

   This fact should help infuse you with faith in yourself and God. He has been orchestrating people, events, and geographic locations to help you get to your destiny. That is why the Scripture Romans 8:28 should never get old for us: *"And we know that in all things God works for the good of those who love him, who have been called according to his purpose."* God used the midwives to save the lives of many babies, including Moses, and their fear of the Lord set them up to receive their own blessing from Him. The text says that God gave them families of their own.

2. **God will bless the people who are a blessing to you!**

   My husband and I recently started a church. I am constantly in awe of the people who share praise reports of things God does for them after they give, serve, or pray with us. What if we had never started? What if we were too afraid? What if we let some of our past church experiences keep us from obeying God's voice? If we had not stepped out, all of us would have missed out on the blessings we have individually and corporately received.

   Now, if we fast forward to Exodus 3, we see God appear to Moses. Verses 7-12 show the dialogue that proves Moses was initially not having any of it: *"7 The Lord said, "I have indeed seen the misery of my people in Egypt. I have heard them crying out because of their slave drivers, and I am concerned about their suffering. 8 So I have come down to rescue them from the hand of the Egyptians and to bring them up out of that land into a good and spacious land, a land flowing with milk and honey—the home of the Canaanites, Hittites, Amorites, Perizzites, Hivites, and Jebusites. 9 And now the cry of the Israelites has reached me, and I have seen the way the Egyptians are oppressing them. 10 So now, go. I am sending you to Pharaoh to bring my people, the Israelites, out of Egypt." 11 But Moses said to God, "Who am I that I should go to Pharaoh and bring the Israelites out of Egypt?" 12 And God said, "I will be with you. And this will be the sign to you that it is I who have sent you: When you have brought the people out of Egypt, you will worship God on this mountain."*

God goes on to give Moses an incredible motivational speech. Yet, Moses doubted himself. Whew! How many of you can relate to this? This encounter is proof that:

3. **After all these centuries later, God sees within us what we cannot see in ourselves.**

In today's time, He uses parents, friends, spouses, teachers, mentors, preachers, pastors, and influencers to help us see ourselves, our gifts, purpose, and callings correctly. Moses was still not convinced by Exodus 4. He proceeds to point out even more of his flaws to God, hoping that he would disqualify himself from the leadership assignment God was appointing him to carry out.

We know the story, and eventually, Moses reluctantly completed his God-ordained mission. Now, I am not hating on Moses. He was an adopted kid raised by his people's murderous enemy. His mother had to abandon him to save his life. His entire life was a lie, and once he learns the truth, he is so full of rage that he murders an attacker and becomes a fugitive. Moses finds solace in a distant land, settles down, and has a family. Then, God taps him on the shoulder to return to the land of all of his anguish. Not only does He want him to return, but He is also giving him the mandate to free the Hebrew slaves from the household who raised him from birth.

That is a tall order for the best of them, but it turns out Moses also had a stutter. Think about anyone you know who stutters; even people who love them laugh or get a little frustrated waiting for them to complete their thoughts.

As we close this section, all of Moses' flaws prove to us that:

4. **God knows our faults, flaws, and pedigree but still chooses us to complete the good work He began in us.**

Let Moses' story encourage you to take up your staff and begin to fulfill your assignment on the Earth.

If you need help getting started, let me tell you what helps me, affirmations. Affirmations are intentional declarations using words to frame the world or reality you wish to create. First, start with an affirmation summary statement. This is a faith-fueled confession that gets you started in the right direction, and then you can create one-sentence affirmations that you say to yourself daily until you can recite it from memory.

This is one of my affirmation summary statements: *"I am aware of my thoughts and will not allow the fears and doubts buried in my subconscious to distract or derail me from achieving my dreams. I will overcome the mental warfare against the enemy by praying more, trusting myself more, and writing more affirmations. Be aware of my thoughts and not let my brain spiral into a negative place on false facts."*

A Set of Affirmations for you to begin:

- I love myself!
- Fear will no longer be a part of my vocabulary or my mindset!
- I want to be close to God constantly!
- I will be a great and outstanding mother/parent to _____!
- I am a great and outstanding wife and partner to _____!
- I will be a great and outstanding friend/family member to _____!
- I am successful and healthy!
- I am a business owner with many opportunities coming my way!
- I will not live inside my comfort zone!
- I deserve all that is happening in my life!

    I will be a millionaire by the time I'm _____, if not sooner!

    I will obtain financial freedom by the time I'm _____, if not sooner!

In the space below, create a set of affirmations that address your fears, help you navigate your faith, and eliminate the false facts attempting to hold you back.

_____

_____

_____

_____

_____

_____

_____

_____

_____

_____

_____

_____

_____

_____

_____

_____

DEVOTION DAY 5:
FORGIVENESS...
THE MOST HATED MEDICINE

As children, we face so many things that this generation will probably never experience. One of those things is horrific-tasting medicine. I remember a few years ago, I saw on the News that pharmacists now had the ability to change the flavor of medicines. I felt like the advancement was important for all patients, but especially children. I don't know about you, but medicine was the least bad-tasting thing you could get stuck with if you had grandparents. From prune juice to cod liver oil, older remedies would take this generation out! The reality of the situation is that we grew up being taught that often, the best things for your health do not always taste the best (like how you probably viewed veggies as a child).

Well, the same is true for forgiveness. I once heard a very honest pastor preach a message. He said, "If we tell the truth, it feels good to hold a grudge." I chuckled on the inside because many of my toughest life lessons have been centered around forgiveness. Eventually, I realized that I became a vessel of bitterness and resentment because I did not know how to forgive. And that's when it occurred to me that for many years, I transformed my inability to forgive into this false perception of "strength." I had been masquerading the manifestations of my inability to forgive, bitterness, and resentment with the "I'm good" or "I don't sweat the small stuff "mentality." This was a mentality that told the world that hurtful actions or words from others did not affect me at all. All this taught me how to harbor bitterness and resentment longer, which made forgiveness much more foreign. It was only when I decided that I was going to improve my quality of life and become a better person that I truly learned how to forgive.

As someone whose life is centered around helping people live healthier lives both physically and spiritually, I now understand why God made sure I took my bitter-tasting forgiveness medicine once and for all. Here are a few reasons why this is vital:

1. **Forgiveness is medicine for your physical body.** In an article by *Seattle Christian Counseling*, a study by Johns Hopkins revealed, "Unforgiveness is linked to higher incidences of stress, heart disease, high blood pressure, lowered immune response, anxiety, depression, and other health issues." Think about that for a second. How you feel about another person can actually rob you of your health. I don't know about you, but nobody and nothing is worth a heart attack, stroke, immune deficiencies, and mental health issues.

2. **Forgiveness affects your other relationships.** Have you ever met someone who holds to the past so tight that they have no room to let the future in? I have. It is one of the saddest things to watch. Too many people wait too long to release their offender; by that time, they have lost weeks, months, and years that they could have spent living a joyous

life. The benefit of applying the healing balm of forgiveness is that it brings positivity to all of the other relationships in your life. You would be shocked at how the other relationships in your life are impacted while you are harboring unforgiveness.

3. **Forgiveness takes root in your soul and enables you to have the most pure relationship with God.** The Word tells us to "forgive" so that we, ourselves, may be forgiven.

Devotional Scripture Day 5
Matthew 6:14-15, NIV

"14 For if you forgive other people when they sin against you, your heavenly Father will also forgive you.
15 But if you do not forgive others their sins, your Father will not forgive your sins."

It is vital to understand that as Christians, forgiveness is essential to our faith. We forgive because we have been forgiven. However, forgiveness should not be automatically connected to access. There are offenses that can be committed to you or against you that can result in someone being eliminated in participating in your life. The elimination of their presence should not be connected to your forgiveness. For instance, when Joseph's brothers sold him into slavery and later needed his help, he forgave them but the Bible never said he forgot what his brothers had done.

Proximity, relationship, and severity of offense should be taken into account when executing forgiveness. People who live in the same house as you should not be treated the same as those you go to work or school with each day. The only exception is abuse; you cannot stay in a relationship with someone who is assaulting you physically, emotionally, or sexually. You must swiftly and strategically remove yourself from these relationships and habitations. For the minor offenses of spouses, parents, friends, and roommates, you cannot allow offense to fester; I caution you to forgive them quickly and often.

The Cycle of Forgiveness

The two hardest parts of forgiveness are:

1. **Making the decision to forgive and identifying what true forgiveness is.** For the sake of our discussion, we will define forgiveness as releasing or canceling a debt of wrongdoing.

2. **Understanding that forgiveness requires repetition.** We must realize that forgiveness is a repetitive behavior that is easier the more you use it, much like weight training and working out. It is difficult when you start, but it grows easier over time.

Devotional Downloads

Once you are aware of the cycle, you can start the journey of forgiveness. Here are some suggestions for you to consider:

1. **Assess the offense:** we must be careful not to major in the minor; however, we also owe it to ourselves not to allow disrespect, mistreatment, or abuse.

2. **Journal the process:** writing down your thoughts, feelings, and emotions can be valuable in processing the path to forgiveness and wholeness.

3. **Enlist support from your inner circle:** whatever you do, do not attempt to take this journey by yourself. Tag in your significant other, family, and friends if appropriate to do so. Also, getting outside help from a pastor, therapist, psychiatrist, or psychologist is sometimes necessary and helpful.

As we end this devotion, I invite you to ask yourselves the following questions and take action to produce forgiveness in your life:

Who do you need to forgive?

_____

_____

_____

_____

_____

_____

Where are you in your forgiveness process?

_____

_____

_____

_____

_____

_____

Who are you requesting to walk with you on this difficult path?

_____

_____

_____

_____

_____

_____

DEVOTION DAY 6:
PUSHING PAST OPPOSITION

As I have gotten older, I have learned that people who remind you of what you are "NOT" or "who you used to be" are often folks who are destined to be a part of your history, but God allows them momentarily to be a part of your present! Those people ask you questions such as:

"How are you going to inspire people when you used to (fill in the blank)?"

"How are you going to go for that job when you don't have that degree or experience?"

"What do you know about running a business?"

"How exactly are you starting your own business?"

"Are you sure you know what you are doing?"

Or you may get asked this one, which is one of my favorites..."*So...when did this change happen?"*

We all are human, and honestly speaking, sometimes other folk's perceptions of who they think you are and should be sometimes limit you from reaching new heights! Unfortunately, I, too, am guilty as charged. The negativity associated with other people's thoughts, opinions, and perceptions shuts us down from sharing our struggles, achievements, and victories.

We allow the perception of others to define us. But see, I don't think these naysayers realize there's a reason why God will enable you to advance to new heights, and they have to watch it happen while questioning YOU the entire time.

Sometimes, God has to do it in front of them to prove them wrong. Other times, He does it to prove to us that He is I AM in our lives, and where we are weak, He is strong. God has shown up for me in some of my weakest moments. He has opened doors for me that I just knew were nailed shut.

Time and time again, He has given me access to opportunities I was not qualified to receive, but God did it anyway! As I have gotten older, I understand why our ancestors would rock back and forth, sing hymns, and walk the floor speaking in their Heavenly language. They knew something that I am realizing more and more: naysayers are part of the trial. I now know that the opposition was a part of the journey and the misery was necessary to obtain the miracle.

And now that I get it, I want to help you shift your mindset quicker and save you some grief and heartache. Sometimes, God will use an enemy to push you to prayer, which is what happens in today's devotional Scripture lesson.

Devotional Scripture Day 6
1 Samuel 1:1-7, NIV

"1 There was a certain man from Ramathaim, a Zuphite from the hill country of Ephraim, whose name was Elkanah, son of Jeroham, the son of Elihu, the son of Tohu, the son of Zuph, an Ephraimite. 2 He had two wives; one was called Hannah and the other Peninnah. Peninnah had children, but Hannah had none. 3 Year after year, this man went up from his town to worship and sacrifice to the LORD Almighty at Shiloh, where Hophni and Phinehas, the two sons of Eli, were priests of the LORD. 4 Whenever the day came for Elkanah to sacrifice, he would give portions of the meat to his wife Peninnah and to all her sons and daughters. 5 But to Hannah, he gave a double portion because he loved her, and the LORD had closed her womb. 6 Because the LORD had closed Hannah's womb, her rival kept provoking her in order to irritate her. 7 This went on year after year. Whenever Hannah went up to the house of the LORD, her rival provoked her till she wept and would not eat."

If you are unfamiliar with this story, please keep reading it at your leisure; the story has a Hallmark Movie ending and not a Lifetime Channel one. In this Old Testament story, Hannah was the favored wife of Elkanah, but she had a problem. She was barren because the Lord had closed her womb. Let that sink in for a minute. She was childless by God's hand. Let this be a reminder to you that sometimes God will make the journey long because He wants to be glorified in your life, and He has a process to produce your miracle.

In this story, we see that Hannah is the beloved wife; she gets double portions and is still unhappy and unfulfilled. She desires to be a mother. But what's worse is that Elkanah's other wife torments and teases her because she is childless. There is a lot of spotlight on bullying today, but it is nothing new. Bullies and mean girls existed even in Biblical times. Hannah teaches us three ways to handle opposition:

1. **She remained grateful for her favor.** At no point in the story do we see her snapping at her husband because of her situation. She remained respectful and loving despite going through a rough time. That is a lesson for all of us not to take out our frustrations on those closest to us.

2. **She did not respond to her antagonist.** Hannah did not curse out Peninnah; she did not give her a 'piece of her mind,' nor did she attack her physically. And for some delivered saints, I know at least one of these would have been an option.

3. **Hannah sought after God regarding her situation.** Hannah went to the temple and prayed so intensely that the priest thought she was drunk! Hannah did not look to the left or right, nor did she call her girlfriends; she went to God, and He heard her prayers.

Devotional Downloads

It is important to understand that God allows opposition. The children of Israel faced Pharaoh's army, but God allowed them all to drown in the Red Sea. David went up against Goliath but emerged victorious! In the same way, God allowed them to face fiery trials and obtain victory, He will do the same for you.

What areas are you facing opposition? In what ways will you partner with God to achieve victory? Consider the suggestions below:

* Dedicated times of prayer
* Going on a fast
* Combining prayer and fasting

Write out your plan here:

_____

_____

_____

_____

_____

_____

DEVOTION DAY 7:
DISCERNMENT VS. INTUITION

We live in a time where mentorship is highly encouraged. Even though mentorship is not an entirely new concept, there was a time when apprenticeship was more common than mentorship. Both are vital, but I want to caution you to be careful of mentors who talk to you more about your potential than your plan. Your potential is wonderful, but it is only evidence of possibility.

I am a proponent of apprenticeship because it is hands-on training and helps you learn through demonstration. If you are going to make good decisions in life, it is critical to be around people who help you understand discernment. Discernment is a crucial aspect of the Christian faith, as it allows believers to distinguish between truth and falsehood, good and evil, and right and wrong. The Bible instructs Christians to test everything and hold fast to what is good (1 Thessalonians 5:21) and to not be conformed to this world but be transformed by the renewing of their minds (Romans 12:2).

Often, discernment can be confused with intuition. The challenge with that is intuition can be fueled by emotions while discernment is achieved through the lens of prayer, and those petitions of heaven result in decisions covered in prayer. It may be confusing because intuition and discernment are two concepts often used interchangeably, but they have different meanings.

Intuition refers to the ability to understand or know something without conscious reasoning. It is often described as a "gut feeling" or a "sixth sense." Intuition is an innate ability that we all possess to some degree, and it can be honed through practice and experience. Consequently, it can be faulty due to emotions and experiences as well.

Discernment, however, requires believers to have a deep knowledge of God's Word and an understanding of His character and purposes. By studying and meditating on the Bible, Christians can develop the ability to recognize false teachings and deceptive practices. It also involves seeking wisdom and guidance from the Holy Spirit, who enables believers to see beyond outward appearances and discern the motives and intentions of others. Discernment is vital for Christians because it helps them to make wise decisions that honor God and align with His will. It allows believers to avoid the pitfalls of sin and temptation and to choose paths that lead to spiritual growth and maturity.

Overall, discernment is a valuable tool for Christians as they seek to live a life that pleases God and reflects His love and truth to the world. The ability to discern is crucial today, where we are constantly bombarded with information and opinions from various sources. Developing discernment allows us to filter out the noise and focus on what is truly important, leading to a more fulfilling and purposeful life.

Devotional Scripture Day 7
#1 - Hosea 14:9, NIV

*"9 Who is wise? Let them realize these things.
Who is discerning? Let them understand. The ways of the
LORD are right; the righteous walk in them, but the rebellious
stumble in them."*

Unless you are Olivia Pope from the popular hit show *Scandal*, it will always be more beneficial for you to use discernment than going with your gut (intuition). Discernment is a word that we do not hear as much in church anymore, but it is really a heightened spirit interwoven with wisdom through a prophetic lens. Christians are taught to believe in the Trinity: the Father, Son, and Holy Spirit. Therefore, the Holy Spirit allows us to glimpse beyond what we see on the surface level, equipping us with supernatural wisdom that ignites prophetic gifting.

Devotional Scripture Day 7
#2 - Philippians 1:9-10, NIV

"9 And this is my prayer: that your love may abound more and more in knowledge and depth of insight, 10 so that you may be able to discern what is best and may be pure and blameless for the day of Christ..."

According to a study in the Blue Letter Bible Commentary, "The gift of discernment of spirits is the ability between spirits that are divine, demonic, or human. This gift helps prevent confusion in the church, for it guards against false teaching. Discernment of spirit should be done on an individual basis as well as being done by the entire church. There are a number of views as to the exact nature of the gift."

It is vital today that we recognize the difference between godly spirits and demonic ones. Our ability to know if the information given to the Body of Christ is spirit-filled and Word-based is also crucial in these last days in which we are living. As we seek spiritual mentors and leaders, we must choose those who can help us increase our wisdom and discernment because too many external forces can influence intuition.

Devotional Downloads

Do you already have a good grasp on the gift of discernment? If yes, how have you used it recently?

_____

_____

_____

_____

If not, what have you learned, and how will you apply it to your Christian walk?

_____

_____

_____

_____

DEVOTION DAY 8:
TAKE THE LIMITS OFF

I remember the first time I heard the song "No Limits" by Israel Houghton. My faith was renewed in a way that I had never felt before. As believers, if we are going to experience a "limitless" life, we must first decide to pack up and leave our comfort zones. I will be the first to admit comfort zones are hard to leave for good reasons. First, it is scary to step outside of them, and fear is real. Fear is an emotion that is often experienced and can be helpful in some situations. However, fear can also limit life and hinder success, happiness, and personal growth.

For example, fear of failure often prevents people from pursuing their dreams and achieving their goals. We all know someone so afraid of failing they may not even try or put in the effort required to succeed. Fear of the unknown is the worst because it prevents us from exploring new opportunities, traveling to new places, or trying new things.

Think about it this way: imagine a man or woman who has won an all-expenses-paid vacation, but they are afraid to fly. The winner has a complex dilemma. They must get on the airplane for the incredible adventure waiting for them. But what happens if they cannot overcome the fear of flying? They forfeit their prize. Now, on the one hand, they are safe. The person did not die in a plane crash, yet they are *so* safe that they are only existing; unfortunately, they have decided to stay neatly tucked away in their comfort zone. So, they are not living their life to the fullest. They are merely surviving and not truly thriving.

Imagine if the same scared person gets on the plane but misses their connecting flight. They can still get to their adventure; they will just be delayed. Some people give up because of a failure or a delay, but people who understand that challenge is sometimes part of the experience won't. Failure is a part of the growth process. You really only fail if you don't learn. And you never learn while stuck in your comfort zone because comfort zones are also "limit zones." *Ouch*, it sounds different if we rename it, doesn't it? Let's look at how limit zones place restrictions on our lives:

1. Limit zones **make us miss new experiences and opportunities.**
2. Limit zones **prevent us from learning new knowledge or skills.** If we don't take the time to learn and develop new skills, we may not be able to pursue particular career paths or personal goals.
3. Limit zones **hinder us from meeting new people.**

Overcoming limitations is essential to confront fear and flee our comfort zones. These actions can include seeking support from friends, family, or a professional and gradually exposing oneself to the feared situation with the help of a therapist. Confronting our fears and eliminating limit zones is vital to achieving our full potential in life.

Fear is one of the most significant hindrances to living a limitless life. If you are constantly battling anxiety and stress, I understand your pain. For years, I allowed these issues to wreak havoc on my mental and physical health. Nothing is worse than being so paralyzed by fear and negativity that you remain stuck in bad situations and cannot make positive changes in life. In the same way God empowered Joshua in the Old Testament, I believe He will also encourage you. So, let's get into today's Scripture lesson.

Devotional Scripture Day 8
Joshua 1:1-6, NIV

"1 After the death of Moses, the servant of the Lord, the Lord said to Joshua, son of Nun, Moses' aide: 2 "Moses my servant is dead. Now then, you and all these people, get ready to cross the Jordan River into the land I am about to give to them—to the Israelites. 3 I will give you every place where you set your foot, as I promised Moses. 4 Your territory will extend from the desert to Lebanon and from the great river, the Euphrates—all the Hittite country—to the Mediterranean Sea in the west. 5 No one will be able to stand against you all the days of your life. As I was with Moses, so I will be with you; I will never leave you nor forsake you. 6 Be strong and courageous because you will lead these people to inherit the land I swore to their ancestors to give them."

Whew! I don't know about you, but every time I read this passage, I get encouraged all over again. For context, the children of Israel have been wandering in the wilderness for forty years because of mumbling, complaining, and a lack of faith. A journey that should have taken them less than two weeks ended up taking four decades. To make matters worse, God did not even let them walk into the promise; He saved it for their children.

At the time of this text, God is providing instruction to Joshua because God chose him to be their leader. In order to walk into the promise, it required an exit from the current comfort zone. We can learn how to get to our limitless promise by applying the directions given to Joshua.

1. **Get ready**: the first thing the people were instructed to do was to prepare. It is too late to prepare once the opportunity arrives. If you are believing God for anything, it is in your best interest to prepare for it. Get in the gym and get your physical body ready. Save money and get your financial house in order. Go to a therapist and heal your emotions before you get a life partner. I *double dog dare* you to prepare for the blessing you are gearing up for, and like our beloved Bishop Jakes would reiterate, "*Get ready! Get ready! Get ready!*"

2. **Set your feet**: to receive this part of the blessing, you have to go where the blessing is because some promises are geographical.

3. **Extended territory**: this blessing is expansive; it is bigger than you can imagine. God has something for you that will blow your mind, but you must leave your limit zone to get it.

4. **Absent enemies**: God told Joshua that no one would be able to stand against him all the days of his life. The same promise is true for us. Our enemies cannot touch us. There is a place

that God has for us where even though the weapons form, they will not prosper.

5. **Be strong and courageous**: God has an inheritance for you, but it will require bravery, grit, and fortitude. Everything you have been praying for is on the other side of your courageous faith, stepping outside the current limit zones!

Devotional Download

From the verses above, which one spoke to you the most? What is your plan to break free from any limit zones currently holding you back?

_____

_____

_____

_____

_____

_____

Honest, Healed, & Happy

DEVOTION DAY 9:
CONFIDENCE—FINALLY, NAILED IT!

In the journey of life, we often encounter habits or struggles that seem impossible to overcome. For me, one of those lifelong struggles has been nail-biting. It's a habit that has plagued me for as long as I can remember, and it's said that the underlying causes are often linked to shame, guilt, and nervousness. However, today, I want to share a personal story of transformation, one that centers around my nails—my real nails—and the profound symbolism they now hold for me. These nails represent not only physical growth but, more importantly, the growth of my confidence and self-belief.

Nail-biting is a common habit that many people struggle with. It often begins in childhood and, if left unchecked, can persist into adulthood. For me, it was a coping mechanism, a way to manage nervousness and anxiety. It was also a silent expression of my inner struggles, a physical manifestation of the emotions I couldn't put into words. I had tried numerous times to quit, but the cycle always seemed unbreakable.

As mentioned earlier, nail-biting is often rooted in deeper emotions like shame and guilt. For me, it was linked to a lack of confidence. I constantly worried about what others thought of me, feared judgment, and felt inadequate. My nails became a canvas of my self-doubt, chewed to the quick by my insecurities.

The journey to breaking free from nail-biting began when I decided it was time for a change. I was tired of feeling self-conscious about my hands, and tired of hiding them in shame. I realized that if I wanted to grow in confidence, I needed to confront this habit head-on. Although a physical habit, there were spiritual reasons for this expression. I quickly realized that breaking a deeply ingrained habit is not easy, and it often requires support. I confided in close friends and family about my goal to quit nail-biting. Their encouragement and understanding played a crucial role in my journey. Having a support system to hold me accountable made all the difference.

As I embarked on this journey, I turned to prayer to God and reflection on His promises. I sought inner strength and guidance to overcome not just the physical habit of nail-biting but also the emotional baggage that had contributed to it. Through prayer, I found solace and a renewed sense of purpose. As the days turned into weeks and then months, I began to see a remarkable transformation in my nails. They started to grow, slowly but surely, as did my faith in God!

The mere sight of my natural nails extending beyond their previously bitten state filled me with a sense of accomplishment. But these nails meant more to me than just a physical change. They symbolized the personal growth and newfound confidence that was taking root within me. Each millimeter of growth represented a step away from self-doubt and toward self-assurance. It was a tangible reminder of my resilience and determination and that if I anchored this journey in the Scriptures, I would be able to tackle other areas of uncertainty by trusting in the intelligence I was created with!

Confidence is a powerful force. It can shape our choices, influence our actions, and ultimately determine our destiny. As my confidence grew, I found myself taking on challenges I had previously shied away from. I spoke up in meetings, pursued new opportunities, and embraced my authentic self without fear of judgment.

One of the most important lessons I learned on this journey is that confidence doesn't mean perfection. It means accepting ourselves, flaws, and all. My nails, though now healthier and longer, still bear the scars of years of nail-biting. They serve as a reminder that growth and confidence are not about erasing our past but about embracing it and using it to propel us forward.

My journey from nail-biting to confidence offers valuable life lessons that we can all apply to our own struggles:

1. **Identify the root cause**: it's crucial to identify underlying causes to conquer a habit or challenge. Understanding why we engage in certain behaviors allows us to address the root issues.

2. **Seek support**: we don't have to face our struggles alone. Reach out to friends, family, or professionals who can provide guidance and encouragement on your journey to personal growth.

3. **Spiritual connection**: prayer and reflection on The Word of God are powerful tools for self-discovery and strength. Connecting with the Lord will give you the resolve to

overcome even the most ingrained habits. Isaiah 41:10 NIV, states, *"So do not fear, for I am with you; do not be dismayed, for I am your God. I will strengthen you and help you; I will uphold you with my righteous right hand."* This revelation strengthened my faith and helped me to understand my value.

4. **Celebrate progress**: acknowledge and celebrate every small step of progress. Whether it's the growth of your nails or the development of your self-confidence, these milestones are worth celebrating.

5. **Embrace imperfection**: perfection is an unattainable goal. Instead, embrace your imperfections as part of your unique journey. They are a testament to your growth and resilience.

In my lifelong battle with nail-biting, I discovered that true confidence isn't about having flawless nails or a perfect exterior. It's about nurturing the strength within, overcoming self-doubt, and embracing our authentic selves. My nails, once a symbol of insecurity, now stand as a testament to the power of determination and self-belief. May this story inspire you on your own journey to confidence, reminding you that with patience, support, and a belief in yourself, you too can say, "Finally, I nailed it!"

Devotional Scripture Day 9
Isaiah 41:10, NIV

"So do not fear, for I am with you; do not be dismayed, for I am your God. I will strengthen you and help; I will uphold you with my righteous right hand."

This verse reminds us that God is always with us, providing strength and support in times of fear and uncertainty.

Devotional Download

Reflect on a challenging situation in your life where you've felt afraid. It may not have been nail-biting, but anything that caused you to lose confidence in yourself, past or present.

_____

_____

_____

_____

_____

_____

_____

How did surrendering the fears to God impact your situation?

_____

_____

_____

_____

_____

_____

How did you experience God's presence and strength during that time? Share your thoughts and feelings, and consider how you can lean on this promise in the future.

_____

_____

_____

_____

_____

_____

_____

DEVOTION DAY 10:
EVERYBODY CAN'T RIDE

Everybody can't ride on your way to your successful destination. Some passengers are such a liability that you have to stop the vehicle and let them off. The more you focus on what you *can't* do, the more of what you *can* do will become a distant memory! This is why I decided to change my scenic route on my journey to destiny. I no longer allow passengers who tell me "No"—there are no more pit stops that hinder my purpose. My vehicle is insured by God! *Watch me work*!!! As I change lanes, I understand that the process requires focus and occasional discomfort. Allow me to explain further.

Life is an unpredictable journey. It is a twisting road that winds through highs and lows, successes and setbacks. Along the way, we gather companions, some of whom are a true source of inspiration, support, and motivation. In contrast, others are mere burdens, holding us back from achieving our full potential. In pursuing our dreams, we must recognize that only some are meant to accompany us on our path to success. With their skepticism and negativity, some individuals can poison our aspirations, causing doubt to creep into our minds and impede our progress.

With determination as our fuel and perseverance as our engine, we should embark on transformative journeys that demand shedding the dead weight of doubters and naysayers. We should refuse to carry the unnecessary baggage of disbelief and pessimism. Their words of 'can't' and 'impossible' reverberate like echoes of a past we should be eager to leave behind. It's time to redefine our itineraries and take a new route unfettered by the chains of others' limitations and inhibitions.

As we embrace this shift, there are a few things we should consider:

1. **Our focus should be on what we can do**. For every limitation we discard, a plethora of possibilities emerge, like blossoms in spring, unfurling their vibrant petals. Let's choose to concentrate on nurturing the seeds of our potential, cultivating a garden of accomplishments that will bloom with the tender care of our dedication. In this garden, the memory of past restrictions fades into the background, overshadowed by the radiant colors of our capabilities and achievements.

2. **The decision to chart a new course isn't without its challenges**. Steering away from the familiar road and venturing into the unknown requires a certain level of discomfort. It demands that we confront our fears and push beyond the boundaries of our comfort zone. As we switch lanes, we must adapt to unfamiliar terrains, recalibrating our mindsets to align with the demands of this uncharted path. Yet, we must also recognize that in these uncomfortable moments, we grow and evolve, developing the resilience and adaptability necessary to thrive in the face of adversity.

3. **Understand the significance of self-belief.** In this journey of self-discovery and purposeful navigation, our vehicles are not just any ordinary means of transport. Instead, they are fortified by an unwavering faith in God—shielded by an unyielding trust in Him. His power provides us with the strength and courage to persevere despite the obstacles that may loom ahead. With our faith serving as a compass and armor, we find solace in knowing that we are protected, guided, and supported, even when the road ahead appears treacherous and uncertain.

Therefore, we should refuse to be shackled by the limitations of our past or the doubts of those who cannot envision the magnitude of our potential. With every turn of the wheel, we are propelled forward by the unstoppable momentum of determination and the unwavering faith that propels us toward our destined endpoint. The words 'no' and 'impossible' serve not as deterrents but as catalysts, igniting our fiery determination to prove that we can achieve the extraordinary.

As we traverse this newly charted path, be mindful of the need to remain vigilant and focused. We should be cognizant of the necessity to maintain a steady gaze on the horizon, never losing sight of the destination that beckons us forward. Every lane change reminds us that progress is not achieved without discomfort and that growth is not attained without challenges. Through the juxtaposition of discomfort and determination, we are sculpted into the best versions of ourselves, honed and refined by the trials and triumphs of this transformative journey.

Devotional Scripture Day 10
Job 42:7-10, NKJV

"7 And so it was, after the Lord had spoken these words to Job,
that the Lord said to Eliphaz the Temanite, "My wrath is
aroused against you and your two friends, for you have not
spoken of Me what is right, as My servant Job has.
8 Now therefore, take for yourselves seven bulls and seven rams,
go to My servant Job, and offer up for yourselves a burnt
offering; and My servant Job shall pray for you. For I will accept
him, lest I deal with you according to your folly; because you
have not spoken of Me what is right, as My servant Job has."
9 So Eliphaz the Temanite and Bildad the Shuhite and Zophar
the Naamathite went and did as the Lord commanded them;
for the Lord had accepted Job. 10 And the Lord restored Job's
losses when he prayed for his friends. Indeed the Lord gave Job
twice as much as he had before."

If you are not familiar with the story of Job, I highly recommend you read the book in its entirety. The Bible tells us that Job was a righteous man who endured an incredibly difficult season of loss. While mourning, he was visited by three friends who gave him unwise counsel. Instead of supporting him in truth, the men inaccurately gave an account of the reasoning behind his suffering. As a result, Job 42:7-10 tells us that God condemned them for their faulty guidance.

Much can be learned from Job's journey and the friends in his vehicle at the time. First, though Eliphaz, Bildad, and Zophar had good intentions, they did not support Job in a way that pleased God. They relied on their own knowledge and provided advice that discouraged Job, who was already mourning the loss of his family, possessions and physical well-being. While experiencing a setback such as Job's, we should be careful with whom we surround ourselves with. Everyone is not equipped to handle the ride or offer sound advice. During these times, we should pray and ask God to comfort us with our needs.

As we navigate the twists and turns of this uncharted terrain, be assured that our vehicles are not solely dependent on our abilities alone. Instead, they are fortified by an unshakeable faith in a higher power, a faith that serves as our guiding light, illuminating the darkest corners of doubt and uncertainty. We must rely on God. With each passing mile, we are propelled forward by the unwavering belief that our destiny is within reach and our purpose is waiting to be fulfilled. As we accelerate toward realizing our dreams, we are acutely aware that our journey is not merely about reaching the destination; it is about embracing the transformation that occurs along the way and evolving into the resilient, tenacious individuals we are destined to become.

So, just like Job, let the doubters fall by the wayside. Let the naysayers fade into the background because our journey is not defined by their limitations but by our unwavering determination to succeed. Relinquish the burden of their skepticism, allowing it to dissipate into the wind as we soar toward the horizon, guided by the unwavering assurance that our vehicles are insured by a force far greater than any obstacle that may stand in our way. As you redefine your narrative and pave a path that is unencumbered by the weight of others' disbelief, let others watch you work! This is your journey and your destiny. Do NOT be deterred.

Devotional Download

Take a moment to consider all the passengers on your current life journey. Is there anyone in particular that should be removed from the ride? If so, how will you go about doing so?

_____

_____

_____

_____

_____

_____

_____

DEVOTION DAY 11:
EXPECTATION –
EXCEEDINGLY & ABUNDANT BLESSINGS

Your blessings are just beginning to pour in and I know that God has more in store for you and your family— exceedingly and abundantly more! Some people may laugh at the ideas and goals that you have for yourself and your family but guess what? *God got you*!!! You don't have blessed *moments*, you have a blessed *life*!

A strong and positive mindset, built on the foundation of faith and an appreciation for the abundance of blessings, can significantly impact the trajectory of your life. This perspective is often reinforced by motivational literature that resonates with its readers. The profound messages within such books can stir the soul and inspire one to overcome obstacles in pursuit of their aspirations. The unwavering belief in the power of perseverance and an optimistic outlook can guide the path to success and personal fulfillment.

The words within these pages are a constant reminder to embrace a warrior mentality. Refuses to succumb to adversity and confronts it with unwavering determination. By adopting this approach, one can conquer the challenges looming large and achieve the goals. In the face of skepticism or ridicule from others, maintaining focus and steadfast determination remains crucial, serving as the driving force that propels one forward.

Devotional Scripture Day 11
James 1:12, NKJV

"12 Blessed is the man who endures temptation; for when he has been approved, he will receive the crown of life which the Lord has promised to those who love Him."

This passage reminds us that it's essential to recognize that numerous trials and tribulations often mark the journey toward success. However, through these struggles, one can cultivate resilience and grit. These attributes ultimately pave the way for the realization of dreams and ambitions. Amidst the tumultuous waves of life, it is imperative to hold onto one's beliefs, nurturing them with unwavering dedication and allowing them to guide the way toward a brighter future.

The understanding that blessings are not merely fleeting moments but an integral part of our existence can be a source of profound gratitude and humility. With this realization, one can fully appreciate the generosity of the blessings that continuously flow into one's life. This understanding further strengthens the resolve to embrace life's challenges, knowing that every obstacle presents opportunities for growth and personal development.

The acknowledgment that life's journey is not devoid of difficulties underscores the importance of savoring every moment of triumph and joy. Each milestone achieved, and every battle won is a testament to the strength and resilience within. Through these moments, one can truly comprehend the depth of their capabilities and potential for growth.

This book is a testament to the profound impact of unwavering faith, resilience, and optimism in navigating life's tumultuous waters. It encourages readers to steadfastly hold onto their beliefs and embrace the challenges that come their way, with the unwavering certainty that they possess all the necessary tools to overcome any obstacles and flourish in the face of adversity.

Through the lens of this book, one can perceive life not as a series of fortunate occurrences but rather as a continuous stream of blessings, each contributing to the fabric of a rich and purposeful existence. By internalizing the essence of these teachings, individuals can cultivate a mindset that propels them toward a life marked by abundance, growth, and fulfillment.

Devotional Download

What blessing(s) are you expecting God to perform right now? What are your expectations for Him one year from now? Ten years? Explain below.

_____

_____

_____

_____

_____

_____

Honest, Healed, & Happy

DEVOTION DAY 12:
USE WHAT YOU HAVE

The biblical narrative in Exodus 4:1-6 offers profound insights into the theme of using what one has in the service of a higher purpose. In this passage, Moses, a reluctant messenger, grapples with doubts about his ability to convince the Israelites of God's appearance to him. God responds with a powerful lesson on utilizing the ordinary for extraordinary purposes. This timeless message resonates with us today, encouraging us to discover and deploy our latent potential. In this exploration, we will delve into the narrative and extract life applications, culminating in a transformative activity to embrace and use what we already possess.

Devotional Scripture Day 12
Exodus 4:1-6, NIV

"1 Moses answered, "What if they do not believe me or listen to me and say, 'The Lord did not appear to you'?" 2 Then the Lord said to him, "What is that in your hand?" "A staff," he replied. 3 The Lord said, "Throw it on the ground." Moses threw it on the ground and it became a snake, and he ran from it. 4 Then the Lord said to him, "Reach out your hand and take it by the tail." So Moses reached out and took hold of the snake and it turned back into a staff in his hand. 5 "This," said the Lord, "is so that they may believe that the Lord, the God of their fathers—the God of Abraham, the God of Isaac and the God of Jacob—has appeared to you." 6 Then the Lord said, "Put your hand inside your cloak." So Moses put his hand into his cloak, and when he took it out, the skin was leprous—it had become as white as snow."

Moses, standing before God with his staff, symbolizes the standard tools and abilities each person possesses. When God asks, "What is that in your hand?" it prompts us to reflect on our skills, talents, and resources. Often, we underestimate the power within us, just as Moses might have overlooked the significance of his simple shepherd's staff.

Later, God instructed Moses to throw his staff on the ground, where it transformed into a snake. The snake represents the unexpected and transformative potential hidden within the ordinary. Moses, initially afraid, learns to overcome his fear and trust in God's guidance, grasping the snake and witnessing its return to a staff. The narrative emphasizes the significance of faith through Moses' actions. God orchestrates these symbolic acts to prove His presence and power. The leprous hand turning back to normal illustrates faith's transformative and healing nature in action.

God's ultimate goal is for others to believe in His presence through Moses. In our lives, effective communication of our beliefs and values is vital. Moses' experiences serve as a metaphor for our role as messengers, tasked with sharing our convictions in a way that resonates with others. God's message was not just for Moses but for the entire community of Israel—including you! You have been grafted into this beautiful narrative. Similarly, our transformative journeys can inspire and uplift others. By sharing our experiences, we contribute to building a community where everyone is encouraged to use their unique gifts for a greater purpose.

The narrative of Moses and the staff serves as a profound reminder that there is extraordinary potential within ordinary lives. By recognizing, embracing, and utilizing what we already have, we can embark on transformative journeys that impact our lives and inspire and uplift those around us. Through intentional actions and shared experiences, we contribute to building a community where the power within each individual is acknowledged and celebrated. Just as Moses learned to use his staff, may we discover and unleash the unique gifts and potential within ourselves for the greater good.

Devotional Download

Exercise #1

Develop a personal narrative that communicates your beliefs or values. This could be through writing, storytelling, or creating a visual representation. Consider how your unique experiences and journey can inspire and influence those around you. Don't overthink it. Use Google if you need inspiration!

_____

_____

_____

_____

_____

Exercise #2

Identify an area in your life where you need to exercise faith. It could be a personal challenge, a relationship, or a career decision. Take intentional steps toward positive change, trusting that the transformative power of faith can bring healing and restoration. This could be as simple as learning to stick with a realistic budget or walking away from a toxic relationship or habit. This may mean getting a licensed professional counselor on board or joining a support group either virtually or in person. This will take courage, but you've got this!

_____

_____

_____

_____

_____

Exercise #3

Step out of your comfort zone by taking a small risk. This could be volunteering for a task you usually avoid or trying a new skill. It could be volunteering at an organization that champions a cause that matters to you. Embrace the uncertainty and trust that, like Moses' staff, your capabilities can transform and adapt. You have something to offer the world!

_____

_____

_____

_____

Exercise #4

Take a moment for self-reflection. Identify and make a list of your skills, talents, and resources—both tangible and intangible. Acknowledge the potential within, even if it seems commonplace. Once you have those listed, think of creative ways to incorporate these into your life. Granted you have made room by eliminating time wasters like excessive scrolling, TV watching and whatever else that used to take up this time.

_____

_____

_____

_____

_____

DEVOTION DAY 13:
THE ISOLATION TRAP

D estiny is not a solo project. Destiny is not an *"I got this by myself."* When you have an isolated approach to living or reaching your destiny, you miss the opportunity to allow other great people to flock together with you without being intimidated by their greatness. Do you see them through the lens of competitiveness, or are you strong enough to see them through collaboration? Indeed, great people can accommodate the greatness of others. Only insecure people have to shoot down every other great person to function because they fear that if people see options, they will be excluded. Therefore, DON'T BE GREAT BY YOURSELF!!! When you do, you diminish your impact and lose your protection!

Destiny, in its true essence, is not a solitary pursuit. It's not about an individual's triumph or a personal conquest. Instead, it embodies the collective aspirations and collaborations of remarkable individuals journeying together. When one chooses the path of isolation, the chance to attract and embrace other exceptional beings is lost, leaving behind an opportunity for communal growth and shared accomplishments. How do you perceive these individuals? Through the narrow lens of competition, or with the strength to embrace a collaborative perspective?

Truly great individuals possess the capacity to accommodate the greatness of others. Only the insecure find solace in diminishing every other exceptional soul, driven by the fear that multiple options might render them obsolete. But this fear is unfounded. Remember, the brilliance of one does not negate the brilliance of another. Our light doesn't diminish when we stand alongside other luminaries; it only brightens the path for a collective radiance.

Devotional Scripture Day 13
1 Corinthians 12:4-11, NKJV

"4 There are diversities of gifts, but the same Spirit. 5 There are differences of ministries, but the same Lord. 6 And there are diversities of activities, but it is the same God who works all in all. 7 But the manifestation of the Spirit is given to each one for the profit of all: 8 for to one is given the word of wisdom through the Spirit, to another the word of knowledge through the same Spirit, 9 to another faith by the same Spirit, to another gifts of healings by the same Spirit, 10 to another the working of miracles, to another prophecy, to another discerning of spirits, to another different kinds of tongues, to another the interpretation of tongues. 11 But one and the same Spirit works all these things, distributing to each one individually as He wills."

The hallmark of exceptional leadership lies in the ability to recognize the talents and gifts in others, harness their potential, and create a synergy that propels all toward a shared vision. This Scripture reminds us that although God gives us all abilities, there is only one body of Christ. We all have a part to play in the

Kingdom of God. Considering this, there should be no hesitation in allowing a fellow teammate to shine. In this journey, there is ample space for every individual to triumph and contribute meaningfully. The narrative of competition must give way to a narrative of collaboration and shared success.

Isolation, in the pursuit of destiny, is a difficult choice. It leads to an illusionary sense of self-sufficiency, culminating in despair and exhaustion. Pursuing destiny demands a collective effort, an interconnected web of support, mentorship, and collaboration. Embracing the strength of unity doesn't dilute individual impact; it fortifies the collective strength and safeguards against the perils of isolation.

The journey toward destiny is not a solo voyage; it's a tapestry woven from the diverse threads of numerous lives and aspirations. We can create a mosaic of accomplishments, each contributing to a larger, unified purpose. So, let us shatter the shackles of isolation and forge a path where the brilliance of one amplifies the brilliance of many. Let us embark on this journey not as solitary travelers but as a community bound by the shared aspiration of creating a brighter, more vibrant destiny for all.

Devotional Download

Fellowship with other believers is vital for Kingdom-impact. We cannot do life alone—we are stronger together. Have you been trapped in the isolation trap? Who is God calling you to reconnect with today?

_____

_____

_____

_____

_____

_____

_____

_____

DEVOTION DAY 14:
BACK TO THE BASICS

It amazes me how many folks between the ages of twenty-five and thirty-five (millennials) think they have life all figured out. This lifespan is just the beginning, but for some odd reason, millennials believe buying a house, getting married, having children, getting endless degrees, or having a job title equates to wisdom! Though an opinionated generation, many have confused these opinions with facts, translating to wisdom in their millennial minds. However, this cannot be further from the truth! Wisdom comes with TIME after walking a long life journey.

We have created a rat race around goals, as I mentioned above. Still, we need to develop more depth and substance to understand how to maintain these things once we acquire them. We have to get back to the basics: seeking advice from the seasoned generation who have lived life and been married for thirty-plus years. This group includes parents who worked and took care of their families without a degree and created generational wealth without all the technology we have. Following their lead, it is time for us to stop worrying about plateauing and start embracing the journey.

Now is the time to rediscover the essence of life. Let this be your sign to embrace wisdom over impulsive achievement.

Bridging the divide between generations, we realize that we need discipline, technology, loyalty, and innovation for success that benefits the entire community, not just a few rising stars. In the age of fast-paced advancements and the allure of instant gratification, the millennial generation finds itself caught in a paradox. Despite the abundance of information at our fingertips, the true essence of wisdom often eludes us. Pursuing material possessions, societal milestones, and professional accolades has become the cornerstone of our existence, leading us further away from the essence of life. It's time for us to realign our priorities and reconnect with the wisdom that can only be acquired through time and experience.

In our relentless pursuit of success, we've become inadvertently fixated on outward accomplishments, mistakenly attributing them to a sense of enlightenment. The rush to secure a mortgage, tie the knot, and climb the corporate ladder has led many to overlook the profound lessons that only life's journey can offer. We have become a generation obsessed with the 'what' and 'when,' neglecting the 'why' and 'how' that underpin the fabric of existence.

We must realize that true wisdom is not a product of achievements but reflects the understanding gained through life's trials and tribulations. Our predecessors, who weathered the storms of life and built their legacies on the foundation of hard work and perseverance, possess a wealth of knowledge that a mere accumulation of degrees or titles cannot replicate. Their experiences, etched in the annals of time, are invaluable reservoirs of insight that we, as a generation, must tap into.

Devotional Scripture Day 14
Proverbs 1:1-9, NKJV

*"1 The proverbs of Solomon the son of David, king of Israel:
2 to know wisdom and instruction, to perceive the words of
understanding, 3 to receive the instruction of wisdom, justice,
judgment, and equity; 4 to give prudence to the simple, to the
young man knowledge and discretion—5 a wise man will hear
and increase learning, and a man of understanding will attain
wise counsel, 6 to understand a proverb and an enigma, the
words of the wise and their riddles. 7 The fear of the Lord is the
beginning of knowledge, but fools despise wisdom and
instruction. 8 My son, hear the instruction of your father, and
do not forsake the law of your mother;
9 for they will be a graceful ornament on your head and chains
about your neck."*

Proverbs 1:1-9 reminds us that there is a pressing need to reevaluate our priorities and embrace the wisdom that can only be gleaned from the seasoned veterans of life. We must acknowledge that pursuing knowledge and experience is not solely confined to academia or professional success. It transcends these boundaries and resides within the realms of human connection, empathy, and a profound understanding of the intricacies of human existence.

The essence of life lies not in the rat race of achieving societal milestones but in the introspective journey that enables us to comprehend the intricacies of our existence. We must return to the basics to rekindle the lost art of seeking guidance from those who have weathered the tides of time and emerged with a profound understanding of life's fundamental truths.

As we navigate the complexities of modern living, let us not lose sight of the invaluable lessons that our predecessors can impart. Their guidance can illuminate our path and help us navigate challenges. Let us shed the facade of all-knowing arrogance and embrace the humility of acknowledging the depth and breadth of wisdom only time can bestow.

In embracing the journey, we realize there is nothing new under the sun. Through this acknowledgment, we can begin to appreciate the value of the wisdom passed down through the ages. Let us step away from the frantic pursuit of superficial achievements and turn our gaze towards the beacon of wisdom that shines brightly within the hearts and minds of the seasoned generation. Only through this introspection and reverence for the lessons of the past can we hope to forge a meaningful and fulfilling future.

Devotional Download

When was the last time you fellowshipped with an elder? What knowledge did they share with you? If you can't recall your last encounter, make an effort this week to reconnect with a predecessor in your life. Write down their words of wisdom below.

_____

_____

_____

_____

_____

_____

_____

_____

DEVOTION DAY 15:
GODLY CONFRONTATION

Before we unveil the strength of spiritual guidance, we must define godly confrontation. There are two types of confrontation: spiritual and physical. Many people think of the word "confrontational" in the physical sense, thus categorizing individuals who are physically confrontational as strong when, in actuality, they are weak. Weak individuals have to get ANGRY to become confrontational; this is why they struggle to become spiritually confrontational. Why? Because becoming spiritually confrontational has nothing to do with physical confrontation (involving another person) or anger. Instead, it means confronting or checking *oneself*!

It is often difficult to confront our issues and the version of the story we have told ourselves (and everybody else). Ultimately, anger limits our ability to become spiritually confrontational. Anger is simply a plug for a flat tire when you know you must go to Good Year and buy a new one. Anger is a temporary fix.

We cannot allow the mask of physical confrontation to fool us into thinking that we are "real ones." Instead, real ones confront themselves. They return to their story version and say, "Maybe I got that wrong." When we stop living in denial about issues and start confronting our shortcomings, progress will follow. If we don't become spiritually aggressive, we will never be able to walk the path God has planned for us.

Confrontation is often associated with conflict and struggle, yet its true essence transcends physical altercations and heated arguments. While many perceive aggressive behavior as a display of strength, the spiritual confrontation embodies resilience and courage. It is a journey that requires individuals to face their inner demons, challenge their preconceived notions, and embrace vulnerability as a gateway to self-improvement. Spiritual confrontation beckons one to confront one's shortcomings, biases, and misconceptions, catalyzing personal growth and spiritual enlightenment.

In today's world, confrontation has been primarily misconstrued, with physical confrontations glorifying as displays of dominance and power. Society often lauds individuals who resort to aggression and hostility, deeming them strong and assertive. However, this superficial perception fails to recognize the underlying weakness that propels such behaviors. In truth, it is often the emotionally frail who rely on anger and aggression as a means of coping with their insecurities and inadequacies. Their inability to confront themselves on a deeper, spiritual level leaves them trapped in a cycle of destructive behavior and emotional turmoil.

Spiritual confrontation, on the other hand, demands a profound level of self-awareness and introspection. It calls for an unwavering commitment to self-examination and an honest appraisal of one's actions and beliefs. This form of confrontation necessitates a willingness to:

1. **Challenge one's narrative**
2. **Question long-held convictions**
3. **Acknowledge the possibility of personal fallibility**
4. **Humbly approach life's complexities**
5. **Take personal accountability**
6. **Embrace moral integrity**

The journey of spiritual confrontation is not without its challenges. It requires individuals to dismantle their emotional barriers and confront the uncomfortable truths that lie within. This process demands profound emotional maturity and resilience as individuals grapple with their deepest fears, insecurities, and traumas. It is a path that necessitates a willingness to embrace vulnerability and surrender the pretenses that shield one from confronting one's true self. Through this transformative process, one can shed the layers of falsehood and emerge as a truly authentic and spiritually enlightened individual.

Devotional Scripture Day 15
Proverbs 29:8-11

"8 Scoffers set a city aflame, but wise men turn away wrath. 9 If a wise man contends with a foolish man, whether the fool rages or laughs, there is no peace. 10 The bloodthirsty hate the blameless, but the upright seek his well-being. 11 A fool vents all his feelings, but a wise man holds them back."

Including Proverbs 29:8-11, the Bible includes many passages of Scripture that reveal the consequences of unchecked anger. Anger, often seen as a natural response to confrontational situations, hinders the pursuit of spiritual confrontation. It clouds one's judgment and impedes engaging in meaningful introspection. Like a temporary fix for a more significant issue, anger merely serves as a band-aid, masking the underlying vulnerabilities and inhibiting the healing process. True spiritual confrontationalists recognize the futility of anger and instead strive for emotional equilibrium, harnessing their inner strength to address conflicts with grace, empathy, and understanding.

In faith and spirituality, the journey of spiritual confrontation is paramount in fostering a deeper connection with the divine. It is a process that transcends human limitations and delves into the realms of the soul. Those who embark on this journey recognize that spiritual growth necessitates an unwavering commitment to self-improvement and a profound accountability to God. By confronting their innermost struggles and striving for spiritual alignment, individuals can pave the way for a more meaningful and purposeful existence guided by their divine plan.

Ultimately, spiritual confrontation beckons individuals to embark on a transformative journey of self-discovery and personal growth. It is a call to transcend the superficial confines of physical confrontations (such as anger) and embrace the profound strength of confronting one's innermost struggles and fears. Through this process, one can pave the way for a more authentic and purposeful existence grounded in spiritual enlightenment and guided by the divine wisdom of God.

Devotional Download

Which type of confrontation do you have more experience in: spiritual or physical?

_____

_____

_____

_____

How has anger played a role in the way you handle confrontation?

_____

_____

_____

In what ways will you start utilizing the tools discussed in this chapter?

_____

_____

_____

_____

Honest, Healed, & Happy

DEVOTION DAY 16:
REST & RECHARGE

In our fast-paced world, rest is often seen as a luxury rather than a necessity. We prioritize productivity and efficiency over taking care of our bodies and minds. However, restlessness can lead to physical, mental, and emotional burnout. Psalm 127:2 reads, "It is in vain that you rise up early and go late to rest, eating the bread of anxious toil; for he gives sleep to his beloved." This verse reminds us that God provides rest as a gift to those who trust Him.

Physical rest is more than just the absence of activity; it involves intentional practices that promote rejuvenation. God designed our bodies to need rest, and science supports the idea that sufficient sleep and relaxation contribute to overall health. As we prioritize our physical well-being, we honor the temple God entrusted us (1 Corinthians 6:19-20).

Balancing work, relationships, and personal pursuits is a challenging yet vital aspect of maintaining health. God calls us to steward our time wisely (Ephesians 5:15-16). Setting boundaries, learning to say 'no' when necessary, and prioritizing self-care contribute to a more balanced and fulfilling life.

Trusting in God's provision for rest involves surrendering our anxieties and uncertainties to Him. In Philippians 4:6-7, we are encouraged, "Do not be anxious about anything, but in every situation, by prayer and petition, with thanksgiving, present your requests to God. And the peace of God, which transcends all understanding, will guard your hearts and your minds in Christ Jesus."

Caring for our well-being is a comprehensive journey encompassing physical, mental, and spiritual dimensions. In accordance with 3 John 1:2, God's divine desire is for us to flourish in every facet of life. Embracing a holistic approach involves recognizing rest as a sacred gift and prioritizing our health, aligning with God's intention for an abundant life.

Addressing physical health means nourishing our bodies through balanced nutrition, regular exercise, and sufficient rest. Mental well-being entails fostering positive thoughts, managing stress, and seeking emotional support. Spiritually, it involves cultivating a meaningful connection with God through prayer, meditation, and spiritual practices.

Devotional Scripture Day 16
Matthew 11:28, NIV

"Come to me, all you who are weary and burdened,
and I will give you rest."

Not only does rest help us physically recharge, but it also helps us spiritually refocus. In Matthew 11:28, Jesus extends a loving invitation. Here, we find a compassionate Savior who understands the weariness of our earthly journey and offers a divine remedy—rest in Him. This spiritual rest is not just a cessation of physical activity but a profound soul rejuvenation.

Matthew invites us to find rest in Jesus, acknowledging our burdens are shared and lightened through Him. In the busyness of life, it's easy to lose sight of our spiritual well-being. Taking intentional breaks for prayer, meditation, and Scripture reading allows us to refocus on God and find strength in His promises.

By understanding rest as a divine gift, we acknowledge its role in rejuvenating our bodies and minds. Prioritizing health becomes an act of stewardship over the temple God has entrusted to us. This alignment with God's intention for abundant life involves honoring the intricate balance of our physical, mental, and spiritual dimensions.

In embracing this holistic perspective, we acknowledge that our well-being is interconnected and reflects the divine harmony God desires for us. Through intentional care for ourselves, we honor the gift of life and align with God's plan for us to thrive in body, mind, and spirit.

Devotional Download

I've curated a few worthwhile life application activities to help seal what you've learned in this chapter. I believe they will be helpful as you are becoming a better version of you! As we engage in these life application activities, let us remember that rest is not a sign of weakness but a demonstration of trust in God's provision. In the rhythm of rest and recharge, we discover a deeper connection with our Creator, experiencing the fullness of life He intended for us. May we embrace the gift of rest, allowing it to transform our lives and draw us closer to the One who is our ultimate source of strength and renewal.

Life Application Activity
#1: The Balancing Act

This exercise will require your favorite journal, a writing instrument, and a little bit of time.

Boundary setting:

1. Evaluate your current commitments and responsibilities.
2. Identify areas where you may be overextending yourself.
3. Be truthful.
4. Practice saying 'no' to non-essential tasks or commitments that hinder your well-being. You may not know this at first, but as you begin to be honest with yourself, you will notice how setting boundaries positively impacts your energy and focus.

This is the only life application activity that I would suggest inviting a trusted friend or family member to help you identify these areas where you are overextending yourself. If you cannot trust the people in your life because maybe, like me, they are draining you because you didn't know how to put positive boundaries up, ask God to reveal this to you. Believe what He shows you! This exercise will open your eyes and bring lots of clarity.

Life Application Activity
#2: Holistic Health Plan

Develop a holistic health plan that includes physical exercise, a balanced diet, intentional rest, and spiritual practices. Set realistic goals for each aspect and track your progress over a month. Reflect on how this integrated approach positively impacts your overall well-being. This doesn't have to break the bank. Many licensed professionals are giving away this type of advice on social media (especially YouTube) through podcasts, newsletters, and free downloads. Yes, there are also subscriptions and support groups as well. Anyone can do this, so don't make any excuses here! You can do this!

Life Application Activity #3: Prayer Journaling

Start a prayer journal to document your concerns, worries, and prayers. It doesn't have to be fancy with doodles and bullets that are elaborately color-coded (unless you're into that sort of thing). Merely take time each day to bring these before God, expressing gratitude and seeking His guidance. Reflect on how this practice deepens your trust in God's provision and brings peace to your heart. That is the central focus. No bells or whistles are needed. It is just a documentation of what you need from God, what you believe He said, or how the prayer was answered. This is a cathartic practice that gives you a place of release and reflection. Always date the request and the answer. This will help build your faith in the most surprising ways... trust me!

DEVOTION DAY 17:
THE NECESSITY OF BALANCE

God created us to live a life of balance .Just as there is a time for everything and a season for every activity under the heavens ,there is also a time for work and rest .We were not designed to be constantly on the go without taking time to recharge and refocus.

Balance is not just about finding equal time for each aspect of our lives. Still, it's about prioritizing what's most important in each season. It's about learning to say "No" to specific activities or commitments that may be good but not necessary in the current season of life. God calls us to seek balance and rest in Him.

In the intricate tapestry of life, we often find ourselves entangled in the myriad threads of responsibilities, aspirations, and relationships. The relentless pursuit of success in our careers, the cultivation of meaningful connections, and the preservation of our physical and mental well-being create a complex mosaic of demands. However, amid this intricate dance, it is imperative to recognize the profound value of balance.

Devotional Scripture Day 17
Ecclesiastes 3:1, NIV

*"There is a time for everything,
and a season for every activity under the sun."*

This timeless wisdom suggests that life operates in rhythmic cycles, each phase demanding its unique attention. In our quest for fulfillment, we must embrace the divine concept of balance, acknowledging that just as there is a time for work, there is also a time for rest.

The very essence of our existence reflects a divine blueprint that calls for equilibrium. We were intricately designed to navigate the ebb and flow of life, ensuring that our pursuit of purpose is harmonized with moments of repose. The delicate art of balance transcends a mere allocation of time; it beckons us to prioritize the essential facets of our lives, understanding that each season demands a tailored response.

In our dynamic journey, balance becomes a compass guiding us through the labyrinth of competing priorities. It encourages discernment, empowering us to utter a strategic "no" to activities or commitments that, while commendable, may not align with the current season of our lives. This intentional curation allows us to channel our energy and focus toward what truly matters, fostering a sense of purpose and fulfillment.

God, in His divine wisdom, invites us to seek this elusive balance and discover rest in Him. The life of Jesus serves as a poignant example, as He frequently withdrew to solitary places to commune with God. Jesus extends an invitation to all who are weary and burdened, promising rest for the soul. This divine rest is not an exemption from life's challenges but an assurance that, in the pursuit of balance, we find solace in the gentle guidance of a loving Creator.

In the pursuit of balance, trust in God's timing becomes paramount. Recognizing that each season has its purpose allows individuals to navigate transitions with grace, embracing the inherent rhythm of life. By prioritizing what is truly important and finding rest in God, individuals honor the divine design and foster resilience, serenity, and a profound sense of purpose.

In conclusion, the divine wisdom embedded in Ecclesiastes 3:1 beckons us to dance to a balanced rhythm in the symphony of life. Through intentional choices and a deep connection with God, we can craft lives that reflect harmony and purpose, embodying the timeless truth that there is a time for everything under the heavens.

Devotional Download
Life Application Activity: Life Balance Wheel
Feel free to be as basic or as creative as you want. If you want, you can get construction paper and create this wheel; if you have graphic design skills, you can jump on a platform like canva. com, write it down, or attempt a drawing. It doesn't need to be perfect; make it your own. You could even put the info into a spreadsheet. The point is to measure these areas and check and see where to make the adjustments to the new you!

- Reflect on key life areas: Spiritual Growth, Relationships, Health, Finances, Work, Hobbies, and others, as indicated in the Life Balance Wheel.

- Rate each area from 1-10 (1 being unsatisfactory, 10 being excellent).

- Connect with God in prayer, seeking His guidance for balance.

- Devotional Note: Trust in God's plan; aligning your life with His purpose brings true balance.

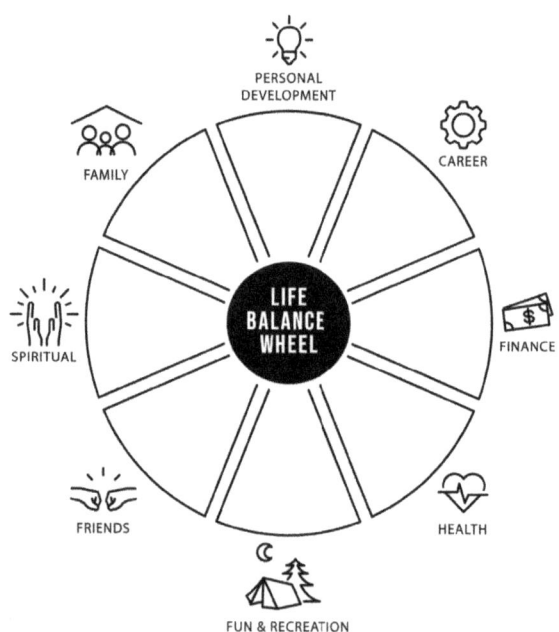

DEVOTION DAY 18:
PRIORITIZING YOUR PHYSICAL TEMPLE

Reflecting on our current habits is pivotal in surrendering our lives to God. As stewards of the bodies entrusted to us, this introspection allows us to align our choices (adjustments) with God's purpose. By assessing our habits through the lens of honoring our bodies as temples of the Holy Spirit, we actively participate in the divine plan, fostering a harmonious connection between our physical well-being and spiritual surrender. This takes us being honest, asking God to show us our habit blind spots so that we can take inventory of what is working and what is hindering our progress. Do this gracefully, knowing that this is not a time to beat yourself up, belittle yourself, or wallow in regret. However, it's a chance to become a new you!

Now, you may be wondering exactly how to achieve that and where to start. I've got an answer for you! Day 18 is not meant to be a comprehensive "how-to" guide. However, I have unlocked some keys that will jump-start you. *Let's dig into it!*

#1- Focus on getting healthy on a budget. We all agree that food costs are at an all-time high. You can maximize savings at the grocery store with these hacks. Before we get into the hacks, ask yourself how much food you are wasting that is being tossed into the trash? It is critical to figure it out because this is wasteful. Also, ask yourself if you need to cook smaller meals?

Now that you have thought through what you need to buy, we are ready to shop! First, create a shopping list to avoid impulse purchases. Utilize loyalty programs and digital coupons for discounts. Opt for store brands and bulk purchases for better value. Buy seasonal produce and frozen items to maximize cost-effectiveness. Lastly, compare prices and consider shopping during sales or discount periods. Saving money on food purchases is a godly thing. It is good stewardship!

#2- **Have healthy options ready for consumption**! Add your fruit, veggies, nuts, and other nutritious alternatives to replace your chips, popcorn, and cookies! #3- Lastly, **meal prep and batch preparation are vital to nourishing meals without breaking the bank**. Pulling this off looks different for everyone, but if you can prep your food, it will significantly reduce your daily cooking time. For some, meal prep and batch prepping look like cooking full meals. Placing them in containers that can be warmed up quickly is a plus. This method also makes you less likely to grab fast food, which hurts you healthwise and wallet-wise.

Time Boundaries

This is an essential part of my day! Being intentional with protecting myself and my time. Normalizing prioritizing mental health is as crucial as maintaining physical well-being. Consider it akin to routine activities like walking or eating right—destigmatizing the practice. Regular mental health check-ins, especially after significant life events like loss or job changes, are crucial for ensuring overall well-being, much like routine dental care.

Water Consumption

Everyone is not a fan of drinking water. For many, it is not a natural skill; I have to schedule it out. Drink an adequate amount of water throughout the day. The experts usually recommend approximately eight 8 oz glasses per day. Personally, over time, I've noticed I become more fatigued when I don't have enough water in my system! Suppose your body is made up of over seventy percent water. In that case, it's understandable why we need to prioritize water intake each and every day!

Body Acceptance

This is even more of a struggle than I initially realized! I've spent a lifetime figuring out what parts of me I liked and those I didn't like. This was very damaging to my self-esteem. So, I had to learn to love this body with all its flaws because it's the only one I have. Embrace gratitude for your unique body, recognizing diverse shapes, sizes, and abilities. Celebrate the body you possess, avoiding detrimental comparisons. Each individual's physical form is a testament to strength and resilience, fostering a positive mindset toward self-appreciation.

Devotional Scripture Day 18
1 Corinthians 6:19-20, NIV

19"Do you not know that your bodies are temples of the Holy Spirit ,who is in you ,whom you have received from God? You are not your own 20 ;you were bought at a price. Therefore honor God with your bodies".

Our bodies are a divine gift entrusted to us by God. As stewards of this precious gift, we are called to honor and care for them as temples of the Holy Spirit (1 Corinthians 6:19-20). We must prioritize our physical health to fulfill God's purposes for our lives. This involves intentional practices such as healthy eating, regular exercise, proper rest, and seeking medical attention for our mental and physical well-being. We are what we do repeatedly. Our habits reflect what we value, not what we wish for. If we want to see results, we must be consistent in small ways as we gradually learn to improve ourselves.

I like this simple approach: minor adjustments will yield lasting results over time. If we want to lose five pounds, we must cut our calories and workout. A new habit could be walking in our neighborhood for twenty minutes a day after work for one month. Then, after that success, we can plan to only have one dessert a week. Consistency is key. After a while, we can seek to drink one less soda, forget the weekly dessert, and swap ingredients for a healthier version of the same dessert. These new habits, over time, will result in weight loss. You may not need to lose weight, but your issue may be water intake: the same principle applies: minor adjustments over time will yield lasting results.

Devotional Download

Let's embark on a journey to prioritize our physical temples with specific call-to-actions to prioritizing your physical temple .Pick an area where you want to start and check them off as you conquer them.

Hydration

___ Drink an adequate amount of water throughout the day.

___ Pay attention to your body's signals of hunger and fullness.

___ Reflect on how hydration and mindful eating contribute to your health.

Get Active

___ Engage in at least 30 minutes of moderate exercise.

___ Choose an activity you enjoy, whether walking, jogging, dancing, or another exercise.

___ Reflect on how physical activity contributes to your overall sense of well-being.

Sleep Tight

___ Ensure you get a good night's sleep tonight (7-9 hours for adults).

___ Throughout the day, take short breaks to relax and de-stress.

___ Reflect on the importance of rest in maintaining a healthy body and mind.

Mental Health Matters

__ Take a moment to assess your mental well-being.

__ If needed, contact a friend, family member, or professional for support.

__ Reflect on how caring for your mental health aligns with honoring your body as a temple.

As you conclude the life application exercise, take a moment to review your notes and insights. Consider how prioritizing your physical and mental temple aligns with your faith and the call to honor your body as a dwelling place of the Holy Spirit. May this journey inspire lasting habits that contribute to your well-being and fulfill God's purposes. Just remember, you are worth it!

DEVOTION DAY 19:
WEALTH—WE ALL NEED IT!

Many people in our world today are striving to attain wealth .They work long hours ,start businesses ,and invest in the stock market ,hoping to become rich. Entrepreneur is the new Doctor ,and while there is nothing wrong with working hard and being financially responsible ,we must understand that true wealth and prosperity come from the Lord.

It is essential to stand apart from the culture of today that glorifies the grind and makes an idol out of personal effort. This mindset eliminates the dependency that God desires for us to have on Him. Sure, He has commanded us to work. However, God's original intent was for us to rule the land and prosper from the fruit of it, not to have every step we take be dictated by the "almighty dollar." God's original intent was for us to put to work all of what He has given us in His hands, work as unto Him, and trust Him for the increase. We should depend on Him for our provision as we work daily.

Now it is very accurate that we need money for everything. Try calling your electric company and telling them to give you an extension on your electricity bill because "God will make a way," and see what happens! As adults, we understand that things cost money, and thus, we have to earn it. Nicer things usually cost more, and you, knowingly or unknowingly, have to choose what level of life you will live.

As believers, we are also responsible for following Christ's teaching regarding the stewardship of our money, like tithing. That principle is taboo in the church today, but it is Biblical and is attached to a promise from God. Your conviction to set aside ten percent of your income for God's house—the church, demonstrates your belief and trust in the financial principles of Christ.

This trust guarantees your provision and supernatural assistance from God, not just financial gifting. It grants you this access even for the intangible needs you may have for God that are impossible to complete no matter how much money you have. This theology is also fundamental to the wealth of us as believers.

Devotional Scripture Day 19
Proverbs 10:2, NKJV

"Treasures of wickedness profit nothing,
But righteousness delivers from death."

The Scripture tells us that the Lord's blessing brings wealth, which is not achieved through painful work for it. This means that God's blessings are the source of our wealth and not our efforts alone. As we seek to honor God and walk in His ways, He is faithful to pour His blessings upon us.

God's blessings often come in unexpected ways, and we must learn to trust Him and not rely solely on our own understanding. As we follow His leading and obey His commands, He will open doors and provide opportunities for us to prosper.

It's important to remember that wealth is not just about money and material possessions. True wealth comes from knowing God and walking in His ways. Wealth is also attached to things that money can never buy, like relationships, physical and mental health, and emotional wellness. As we draw near Him, He will bless us with wisdom, peace, and joy that money cannot buy. So, let us seek God with all our hearts and trust Him to bring true wealth and prosperity.

Proverbs 3:9-10 reads, "9 Honor the LORD with your wealth, with the first fruits of all your crops; 10 then your barns will be filled to overflowing, and your vats will brim over with new wine." Let us be faithful stewards of the blessings He has given us and show our trust in Him by participating in the principles and directions regarding tithing and giving. Then and only then will we have the favor or supernatural assistance from God to enjoy surplus, and again, not just financially. Let us use our financial gain to live better, bless others, and further His Kingdom. Remember, wealth is not just about what we have but who we are and what we have been able to do in Christ.

Devotional Download

The definition of stewardship is the careful management of something. We act as stewards of the time, talent, and treasure God has bestowed upon us. To challenge yourself to donate:

1. Give or exhibit an act of kindness in one of these areas.
2. Pay it forward at your local coffee establishment, or bless an unfortunate person with a financial donation.

3. Offer someone a service of your talent or complete a task for someone else.

4. As you complete this challenge, remember this is an act of service unto the Lord and a representation of who He is to you.

Log the details of your challenge and how you felt in the moment and after.

Additionally, choose a random time while you are working. Be careful to select a time acceptable for your employment duties, such as nursing or monitoring dangerous machinery. Pause from your work to acknowledge God. Thank Him for enabling you to perform your job or complete the duty of which you can. Make a pledge to work the remainder of the day "unto the Lord" or as if you were doing it for God Himself.

Take time to journal the rest of your day. Be sure to note the impact the small moment made on your day.

_____

_____

_____

_____

_____

_____

_____

_____

DEVOTION DAY 20:
SOUL CARE

As we journey through life, we must care for ourselves physically, emotionally, and spiritually. Our soul is the most important part of us, the very essence of who we are, and it requires regular nurturing and care. Neglecting our soul can lead to emotional distress, mental breakdown, and spiritual decay.

Soul care involves taking intentional steps to nourish and replenish our innermost being. It includes praying, reading, and meditating on the Word of God, engaging in activities that bring us joy and peace, and seeking support from trusted individuals when needed.

One meaningful way to care for our soul is through Sabbath rest. This practice allows us to disconnect from the busyness of life and recharge our batteries. Another way to care for our souls is through the practice of forgiveness. Unforgiveness can weigh us down, causing bitterness and resentment to take root in our hearts. Forgiveness frees us from the burden of holding grudges and allows us to experience true peace and healing. Emotional healing, in particular, is so important and affects our overall physical health.

Prioritizing the care of our souls is so important, especially in these two ways:

1. We must seek to nurture it through intentional practices that draw us closer to God and heal up the wounds and bruises that surely come as we live in this broken world.

2. We will experience greater peace, joy, and fulfillment as we prioritize caring for our souls.

When we embrace soul care, we live the life God intends for us to live.

Devotional Scripture Day 20
Mark 8:36, ESV

"For what purpose does it profit a man to gain the whole world and forfeit his soul?"

In the Bible, Jesus reminded us that our soul is of greater value than anything in this world. In Mark 8:36, He asked this question. Here, he wants us to consider the benefit of improper placement of the importance of the soul. This verse reminds us that material possessions and worldly achievements are insignificant compared to the health and well-being of our souls. He teaches us to be careful in what we value by considering the truth of the alternative. Yes, things are important, but consider if you have all the things (tangible) and none of the important stuff (intangible).

Turn on any television show or take the opportunity to ask any person who seemingly "has it all" what is most important to them. The response is usually related to family, friends, and physical health. Dig a little deeper and ask them to focus only inwardly, and you will quickly find out it has to do with their soul. The deep inner working part of who they are. You get responses like my faith in God or my belief in myself. This is an excellent picture to focus on as we pursue all this life has to offer.

God modeled soul care during his documented first act, the creation of everything. After six days of working, He stopped to rest. In Exodus 20:8-10, He commanded His people to keep the Sabbath holy, setting aside a day of rest to focus on

worship and renewal. As we engage in this principle, we allow God to speak to us, heal us, and help us shift our heart posture to explore forgiveness.

In Matthew 6:14-15, Jesus taught us the importance of forgiveness: "For if you forgive others their trespasses, your heavenly Father will also forgive you, but if you do not

forgive others their trespasses, neither will your Father forgive your trespasses." We must care for our souls to live the way God truly intended. He is there to help us do this using rest and forgiveness.

Devotional Download

So, here is where the hard work comes in. Set aside an hour or two of your day. Trust me, you will need this long. Start off with prayer and worship to God, thanking Him for what He has done for you. Dig deep into the intangible things that go unappreciated, like the sharpness of your mind, how your brain works, and how God has gifted you.

As you complete this, take a moment and ask God to show you your faults—particularly in forgiveness. Ask Him to reveal to you any unforgiveness in your heart. This may take a moment of thought, so give yourself time. Be sure to have a piece of paper handy. Write down any names that come to mind. Consider the person who may have hurt, offended, or caused you to hold on to unresolved conflict. Ask God to help you forgive them and release them from the burden of your pain. Christ died for our sins and asked us to forgive others. As you pursue forgiveness, you honor God's forgiveness of your sin.

_____

_____

_____

_____

_____

_____

_____

_____

_____

_____

_____

_____

_____

DEVOTION DAY 21:
BURDENS AND BOUNDARIES

In our fast-paced world, to-do lists crowd our minds. We rush here and there. Do this, do that, go here, and stop by there. We are servants to others we are in relationships with and build our days around their requests. While this is not sinful or ungodly in nature, we do, however, spin our wheels, exhaust our efforts, and sometimes even waste our time on things that have nothing to do with us. We prioritize what others want and need, sometimes placing it over our wants and needs, and our lives, health, and happiness suffer.

Boundaries are, by definition, limits of a subject or sphere of activity. They exist to keep things from going past a certain point, but one thing I have found to be quite revelatory is that boundaries are not always a bad thing. Boundaries keep things within a certain point; this is good. We need things to stay within an area of which they are best suited. For example, the animals in the zoo...umm, they are best suited within the cages they reside in! The boundaries they live in are set and are helpful to keep all of us safe.

In the same way, boundaries are a necessity in life. When set appropriately, they can lift the heavy burdens others bring. Correctly specified and, more importantly, respectfully communicated boundaries are not only beneficial, but they are essential for optimal living. When we set them, we can be and do all that God has called us to do and be and, in turn, be the best versions of ourselves to others.

Do you need to say no to some requests? Do you need to force some people in your life to do some things for themselves that you currently step in and do for them? Do you need to step down from something you should not have committed to or re-prioritize how fast you want to accomplish something, understanding how long it will take? Do you need to set some new time boundaries that will allow you the alone time, reading time, and study time you need to improve? All these things and life assessments are the key to your next level of success.

Devotional Scripture Day 21
Matthew 14:23, NIV

"After He had dismissed them, He went up on a mountainside by Himself to pray."

In this Scripture, Jesus shows us the importance of setting boundaries. Faithful Peter, James, and John were His closest disciples. They walked with Him, pulled on His brain often, and learned from Him. However, we see that Jesus still needed time away from them to be alone. He needed the next level of instruction from God. He needed alone time with the Lord and for God to give Him a resolve before being back with His disciples. They would have questions and need direction and guidance, as we see in the coming Scriptures, as Jesus is about to be taken captive and Peter tries to intervene.

When we create boundaries, give people a "No" when needed, and refuse to interrupt what we have decided we want to set aside time to do, we invite God to prepare for what is to come. We allow God time with us. We give Him space to move in our lives and give ourselves space to prioritize Him.

In the same way, we force those we love most to be better as well, and we teach them how to love us well. We show them the importance of doing what we must do to be at our best for others. We show up for them better. We also invite those around us into the boundary-creating space and teach them how to care for themselves as we care for ourselves in the demonstration.

Create boundaries for your life to protect your time with God and the time you need to be your best self. Do the things you need to do for yourself and help others love you well by calling them to respect your boundaries. Invite them into a life of boundary-setting so that they, too, can live higher.

Devotional Download

You have reached the end of this 21-Day Devotional. Maybe for you, it was challenging to stay consistent. Or perhaps you saw the benefit of daily committing to seek God in this way. No matter which testimony resonates with you, it is essential that as you bring this journey with your devotion to a close, you draw a line in the sand, set some realistic, keepable boundaries for rest (your own personal quiet time), and the time you desire to spend with God.

Today, take a moment to celebrate your completion. Grab a treat for yourself or splurge on a nice lunch or dinner. Often, you will repeat the behavior when you feel celebrated for something you have accomplished. Rewarding yourself naturally for this milestone will give you the motivation to start your next growth journey.

To keep yourself committed to celebrating this accomplishment, document your treat here and how it made you feel:

_____

_____

_____

_____

_____

_____

_____

_____

Next, set aside time to explore what you want your next growth journey to be. Consider how much you have grown in these 21 days. What changes have you made, and what God-breathed revelations have you experienced? Should you start another devotional, find a great book to dive into, or join a community group? The possibilities are endless. Start today on the heels of this victory to plan your next journey. Be specific and schedule all the necessary time to stay consistent and focused.

The next journey I want to take is...

_____

_____

_____

_____

_____

_____

_____

I want to complete this by:

_____

_____

_____

_____

_____

_____

_____

Lastly, *anticipate*. Anticipate what you may ask. Take time and consider all the time stealers, focus grabbers, and things that get in the way of you doing things like a 21-day devotional. If you experience anything in your journey with this devotion, write them down. Benjamin Franklin was the first to say, "If you fail to plan, you can plan to fail." That quote is at least two centuries old and as revelatory today as it was back then! *You have to plan*. Not only do you prepare for what you want to do, but you also have to plan for the adversity, challenges, and struggles that are sure to come against the things you desire to do. Plan for the things in life that surely will come to get in the way of consistency and growth.

As you consider your response from above, please write down your top five challenges (that have happened in the past or are sure to arise) and create a detailed plan to combat them. Do you need to meal prep to save time in the day? Do you need to create a monthly schedule of family meals and shop once a week? As you create a plan to attack the challenges that may arise, you give yourself an exponential increase in potential success. You ensure that you can and will meet your goal. After all, YOU said you wanted to do it right!

Battle Plan:

_____

_____

_____

_____

_____

_____

_____

Potential Challenges

When will this come?

\
\
\
\
\
\
\
\
\

What can I plan to do now to combat this?

\
\
\
\
\
\
\
\
\

TAKE THE NEXT STEP: JOIN THE "HONEST, HEALED & HAPPY" MOVEMENT

You've just completed 21 days of reflection, restoration, and realignment. But this isn't the end—it's only the beginning.

If something in your heart has been stirred...

If you're feeling lighter, clearer, and more connected to God...

Then, now is the time to take the next step.

Join Leslie and a growing community of women committed to living healed, whole, and joyfully aligned with God's purpose.

Say yes to a lifestyle of honest healing and unshakable joy.

Together, we're creating lasting space for transformation—through faith, fellowship, and intentional growth.

You're not alone on this journey.

Tap in. Stay connected. Live healed and happy—on purpose.

Visit **leslieboles.com** and become part of the movement today.

www.ingramcontent.com/pod-product-compliance
Lightning Source LLC
Chambersburg PA
CBHW061656120626
46550CB00003B/962